# 101 Essays to Empower You to Break Barriers

### Frank Agin
Founder & President
AmSpirit Business Connections

**ISBN: 978-1-967521-29-6**

**Published by:**
418 Press, A Division of Four Eighteen Enterprises LLC
Post Office Box 30724, Columbus, Ohio 43230-0724

# Acknowledgement

In sincere appreciation
of Marilyn Agin.

Raising kids takes
patience and love.

Caring for an aging loved
one takes that to a
whole new level.

Hvala!

# Table of Contents

## Look For These Other Books in This Series

*101 Essays to Empower You to Rise & Thrive*
*101 Essays to Empower You to Up Your Game*
*101 Essays to Empower You to Build Momentum*
*101 Essays to Empower You to Limitless Reach*
*101 Essays to Empower You to Elevate Your Influence*
*101 Essays to Empower You to Peak Performance*
*101 Essays to Empower You to The Winning Edge*
*101 Essays to Empower You to Live Unstoppable*
*101 Essays to Empower You to Achieve Greatness*

# Introduction

This book comes from the insight and creativity of Frank Agin.

Who is Frank? He is the founder and president of AmSpirit Business Connections, an organization that empowers entrepreneurs, sales representatives, and professionals to become successful and gain more referrals through networking.

He is the author of several books, including Foundational *Networking: Building Know, Like and Trust to Create a Lifetime of Extraordinary Success* and *The Three Reasons You Don't Get Referrals*. See all his books and programs at frankagin.com.

Finally, Frank shares information and insights on professional relationships, business networking and best practices for generating referrals on the Networking Rx podcast.

In the summer of 2018, he started planning this short-form podcast. As he mapped out what he wanted to bring to an audience of entrepreneurs, sales representatives, and professionals, he knew he'd have hundreds of programs.

But in addition to all that content, Frank noticed he also had a plethora of other materials—instructive, insightful, and inspirational. All this additional content was worthwhile, but none of it was long enough to create a full episode of Networking Rx.

Not wanting the material to go to waste, Frank developed it into short essays—approximately 150 words each. Then he started to record and share those segments daily under the brand Networking Rx Minutes.

For years, he shared a daily message of empowerment, intuition, and hope. This is a compilation of 100 of those essays. Enjoy.

## -1-
## Thoughts To Destiny

There is a short piece floating around the personal development space that goes like this:

Watch your thoughts, for they become words.
Watch your words, for they become actions.
Watch your actions, for they become habits.
Watch your habits, for they become character.
Watch your character, for it becomes your destiny.

There is much truth to this. Think about it. If you flood your mind with positive and optimistic ideas, then you cannot help but verbalize those feelings. And what you say, you tend to do. And do with conviction. And if you did it once, you'll likely do it again. Then three times. Then four. And so on. And what you do over and over serves to brand you as just that. And finally, your personal brand serves to attract similar people, situations, and opportunities to you.

Given this tried-and-true sequence, what's your positive thought for today?

## -2-
## Apples and Seeds

Many notable people have shared one version or another of this phrase: "You can count the number of seeds in an apple, but you can't count the number of apples in a seed."

The average apple contains only about five to eight seeds. But each of those seeds has the potential of becoming a tree. And each of those trees will bear apples season after season. And each of those apples holds seeds to continue the process for eons.

This a powerful notion, but it goes beyond mere fruit. It also has applications to the relationships within your network. You see, when you help another – with an introduction, insight, or opportunity – you move them forward and thus enable them to do the same.

So, do something for another. You are but one person, sure. But your deeds are like apple seeds. They will go on and on and on.

# -3-
# The Compliment Club

In the 1920s, George W. Crane gave the students in his social psychology class at Northwestern University an assignment: Each day for 30 days, students were to give someone – anyone - an honest compliment. He called this *The Compliment Club*.

During this project, not surprisingly, Crane's students noted that their sincere compliments had a positive impact on those around them. Those involved in *The Compliment Club* lifted the people they praised.

When you tell someone, "WOW, you have lost weight and look great," you immediately spur them on in pursuit of shedding the next five or ten pounds. Thus, there is merit in continually looking for ways to lift those around you with well wishes and praise.

Remember that the purpose of compliments is not to make others like you. No! Rather, complimenting others is a form of generosity as it serves to enrich the lives of those around you.

## -4-
## Hold the Door

Next time you head into a building, take a quick glance over your shoulder. If someone is coming up from behind, hold the door for them. It's a simple gesture, but it's one with important and beneficial consequences.

You see, this one small act of thoughtfulness serves as a launching point for other more meaning acts. From this one thing, you've seeded your mind to look for other opportunities to have a positive impact on the lives of other – whether you know them or not.

Soon, you find that you're passing up that prime parking spots so that someone less capable might have it. You randomly smile more at others because you can see the joy it brings them. And then you're sharing compliments when before you might have overlooked the situation entirely.

All of these cascading moments of thoughtfulness simply came from one. Holding the door for another.

## -5-
## Taproot Toughness

In his book *No One Gets There Alone*, sports psychologist Dr. Rob Bell talks about plants with taproots, such as a carrots or turnips. He shares that a taproot grows vertically down as opposed to branching off horizontally. This makes the plant very difficult to displace because it will continue to re-sprout.

He goes on to explain that this plant system is the perfect metaphor for mental toughness. Like the taproot, mental toughness is unseen. It's just there. It's an invisible resilience. It's a tenacity that runs deep. It creates a determination that you cannot displace.

What creates this taproot-like toughness is a clear why. That is, you need to have a compelling reason for working hard. A compelling reason for continuing on, even when success is in doubt. And a compelling reason for driving forth when the end goal is a ways off.

So, think on this: What creates your taproot?

## -6-
## Time or Excuse

Whatever it is you're driving towards, how bad do you want it? Think about it. Be honest with yourself. Do you really want it? If so, what time and attention are you devoting to it.

In his book *No One Gets There Alone*, sports psychologist and mental toughness expert Dr. Rob Bell challenges: "Yes, time is the biggest limiting factor, but it also is an excuse. We all have the same number of hours. If we don't create the time for ourselves, then we simply do not want it bad enough. We either make time or we make an excuse."

Bell's words can be either an affirmation that you're committed, or a wakeup call to double down on your efforts. If it's the former, congratulations.

However, if the latter, ask yourself what needs to change. Examine your days and weeks. There is more time that you think. Find it. Success will follow. And you'll have no need for excuses.

## -7-
## Burn Your Ships

In his book *No One Gets There Alone*, mental toughness expert Dr. Rob Bell shared the story of Hernan Cortez. In 1519, this Spanish explorer arrived at the Yucatan peninsula with 11 ships and approximately 700 sailors and soldiers. They were on a quest to conquer the Aztec empire.

After landing Cortez ordered his men to "burn the ships." Why? He knew that many of his troops had never faced a real battle. The only way they were going to be successful is if they had only one option – to conquer.

Bell goes on to encourage you to metaphorically burn your ships. That is, don't be wishy-washy with respect to whatever you want to do. Rather, take that step – big or small – that commits you to move forward.

No, this doesn't guarantee you success. But it does guarantee that you'll try. And that puts you in the best position to conquer your objective.

## -8-
## The Shelf Life of a Referral

Know this, the business types in your network, love referrals. They're better than cold calls. Less expensive than advertising. And more reliable than just hoping that business will simply appear.

But finding referrals to give is not always an easy task. In fact, some days, finding these opportunities can be a downright daunting task. And, while you may or may not have the opportunity to give referrals every day, you can continually create energy surrounding your referrals in three ways.

One, remind those in your network that you're working on referrals for them and recap generally the things you're looking for. Two, when a referral opportunity presents itself, don't wait. Share that referral promptly. And finally, regarding the referrals you've given, be sure to follow up with those who've handled them and thank them for serving well the referrals you've shared.

Doing these things, gives your referral-giving efforts an extended shelf life.

# -9-
# Just Hang In There

When you think of generosity, you might think of benefiting another by giving tangible objects, such as money or property. Or perhaps, giving someone a referral, important information, or a unique opportunity.

But one of the simplest and easiest means of giving to another is by offering encouragement. Consider this: Everyday, someone around you is enduring a failure, a setback, or some sort of disappointment. Sure, these are an inevitable part of life, as you experience them too.

But that's the point. You can offer tremendous value to someone by sharing that you've stood in their shoes. Remind them that their situation is not unique. Moreover, let them know that there is a way forward. That is what, whatever setback they're experiencing, if they don't give up, life will get better. And you're living proof of it.

So, the treasure you have to offer has value, sure. But encouraging someone to just hang in there is truly priceless.

# -10-
# Get Married to Reasons

In his book *No One Gets There Alone*, sports psychologist and mental toughness guru Dr. Rob Bell shares, "If we look for excuses not to do something, we will find them. However, if we search for reasons why to do something, we can find those as well."

As Bell implies, looking for excuses gives you an escape to a comfort zone. A place where you don't have to try as hard. A situation where your feelings are spared. But it only stands to reason that the notions of excuses and achievement cannot co-exists. That is, with excuses, you cannot achieve. So you want to achieve, you need to divorce yourself of excuses.

Instead, get married to reasons. That is, dig deep into your soul and build an arsenal of motivations as to why you want to achieve. And with these reasons little can stand in your way. In time, achievement will become inevitable.

## -11-
## Small Talk to Big Business

Small talk, in time, eventually transitions to real business talk. And you can artfully make it happen.

For example, if in small talk, someone shares they enjoy water skiing, you might segue with, "Water skiing isn't cheap! What do you do professionally to pay for it?"

Don't try to steer them. Avoid all sales probing. And keep the tone curious and light.

Once the conversation has run its course, touch back on the small talk. For example: "Great talking with you. Assuming, you don't get laid up in the hospital skiing between now and then, I would enjoy continuing our conversation over a cup of coffee sometime."

If you do this, you will have lots of opportunities in the future. Opportunities to do business. As well as opportunities for referrals, introductions, and information. Remember, people do business with those they know, like and trust. And this small talk formula builds it.

# -12-
# Better and Badder

Lewis Howes, lifestyle entrepreneur and high-performance business coach, shared in his book *The School of Greatness*, "Hustle isn't about working smarter instead of harder. It's about doing both. Hustlers are better and badder. They take their place in the world, they don't wait or hope or pray for it to come or for someone to hand it to them.

Howes goes to elaborate that those who hustle have a chip on their shoulder. A swagger about. They work hard and look for ways to become more effective, but at the same time trust and believe that they will make success happen.

How will you hustle today? Do not underestimate the power of it. Hustle brings forth all sorts of opportunity for you. And it also taps into a tremendous amount of your human potential. So, hustle. Commit to – in the words of Lewis Howes - becoming better and badder.

## -13-
## Improve Yourself First

It's easy to see the deficiencies in the lives of others. And to know with seemingly absolute certainty whether they should go left or right in the maze of life. And you feel as if you need to help them.

But, at the same time, you're oblivious your own shortcomings. It's human nature. Yet, the first step in becoming a powerful networker is to get your own life in order.

No, you'll never be perfect. But you can always be better, right? And people want to align with those who are fixated on continual improvement. So, fill in the blank on this sentence: I would like to be better at ...? Think about it.

When you have a clear sense as to what that is, set about taking action to develop yourself. People will be not only be attracted to you but also inspired to improve their own deficiencies.

# -14-
# Copy the Right Cat

On full Networking Rx podcast, professional speaker, sales trainer, and best-selling author Lois Koffi shared, "If you're going to be a copycat, then copy the right cat."

Essentially, Koffi's point is this: It's good to emulate other people. But don't just emulate anybody. Emulate the person who is where you want to be.

And emulate the person who exhibits the strong characteristic and solid principles the resonant with you. Energetic. Optimistic. Friendly. Generous. Encouraging. Open. Honest. And reliable.

Here is the reality, the 'right cat' that Koffi alludes to has already blazed a trail for you to follow. And while your journey might not be precisely like theirs, their example will focus you in the right direction and give you an outline for a successful game plan. You just need to add the hard work and determination.

# -15-
# Under Your Wing

What you likely know is that the best way to get things from your network is to ensure that you are putting things into it. What you might not realize is that a great way to contribute to others is to mentor someone.

Know this: compared to someone else you're likely considered a seasoned veteran of the world. No doubt, you've taken the hard way You've spun your wheels at times. You've made mistakes.

While these may not have been great things for you in the moment, you would be serving another sharing your experience. Take someone under your wing. Offer to answer questions for them. Guide them. Show them how to avoid the pitfalls you hit.

By mentoring another, you are not only helping someone, but you are also contributing to the "greater good" of the community. And this cannot help but serve you well in return.

# -16-
# More Powerful Than Money

Germaine Moody, serial entrepreneur and global connector of influencers, shares in his book The 40 Laws of Networking: "Money cannot work or operate by itself; it must be directed. And clear direction only comes in the form of words."

Moody provides an important insight. The wealth you have right now started from words. Job interviews. Negotiations. Simply asking. All of it involved words – written, typed, or spoken. Without words, there is no money.

He goes on to share that "Words can produce every emotion known to man and instantly instigate any type of resource." Think about it, nothing in your life is more powerful than words. Words are the energy to ignite communication. And from communication great relationships are built.

To be successful, don't focus on money. Rather focus on using words to build bridges with those around you.

# -17-
# One Hundred Percent You

In her book *The Radical Empowerment Method*, professional speaker and personal coach Carrie Verrocchio shared:

"Where you are in life right now is completely due to the choices you have made up to this point. That sounds harsh doesn't it? I know it sounded harsh to me when I began working on this concept in my own life. But harsh or not – it is true. Where you are now is entirely your doing. Where you want to BE – and who you want to BECOME – are also entirely up to you. 100 percent up to you."

Verrocchio certainly dishes out some tough love, right? The fact of the matter is that tough love is generally the truth. You are a product of what you've done or haven't. Your level of achievement is a function of the people with whom you associate.

If you want more from life, it's one hundred percent on you.

# -18-
# Consistency

A man, who is a somewhat overweight and well out of shape, walks into the gym and asks the trainer, "How I can get fit?" The trainer eyes the paunchy man and replies, "Well, there is lots of work to do, but I'd suggest we start with some push-ups and light running." The man replies, Push-ups? Light running? I did those once. They didn't seem to do anything."

That's a comical story, huh? After all, you know that getting in shape is a matter of undertaking physical activity on a consistent basis. And a single bout of a few push-ups and some light running will not suffice.

This same lesson applies to achieving success from networking. Attending a lone event is not enough. Sharing just one value-added post on social media won't move the needle. Having a single conversation over a cup of coffee, won't do it either. Creating networking results that have long-term significance is a product of consistency.

## -19-
## The Three Choices of Challenge

Life is full of challenges and disappointments.  And when you meet with frustrating challenges and disappointing setbacks, life presents you with three choices.

You can completely withdraw and essentially quit. But do you want to associate with that type of person? Of course, not. So don't be that person.

On the other hand, when you meet with challenges and setbacks, you can choose to become jaded and bitter. Again, do you want to associate with this type of person? Heck, NO! You have no interest in having a toxic attitude in your world. So don't bring that into the lives of others.

Finally, when you meet with challenges and setbacks, you can choose to resolve that you will find a way to overcome. And then adopt the actions to make that happen. Do you want to associate with this type of person? Of course. So become this person. In short, become the person you want to associate with.

## -20-
## Shout Into a Canyon

One of the most powerful things you can do in any relationship is show appreciation. That is, show gratitude for who someone is. Or express admiration for what others have done.

Think about it. Share in an e-mail or include in a sentence the phrase, "I appreciate you for ..." and then fill in the words that follow. Whatever they are. Everyone has something for which you can be grateful. Seize upon it and express your feelings.

Sharing that appreciation is like shouting into a canyon. The words go out. And for a moment there is silence. Then in time, whatever you've expressed comes back to you. Again. And again.

When you take the time to share words of appreciation with another, you make them feel special. You up lift them. And they cannot help but feel a sense of appreciation towards you. It won't be immediate, but your gesture will come back to you. Up lifting you in return.

# -21-
# Inescapable Mutuality

Dr. Martin Luther King, Jr., an advocate of peaceful activism and an iconic leader in the American civil rights movement shared, "Injustice anywhere is a threat to justice everywhere. We are caught in an inescapable network of mutuality, tied in a single garment of destiny. Whatever affects one directly, affects all indirectly."

Certainly, King's words were directed towards racial injustice, but they also have broader application. There are seven billion people on the planet, but just one network. We're all connect, either directly or somehow indirectly.

Thus, in reality, thoughts and actions a world away – in time – impacts your life. And as such, your thoughts and actions – in time – impacts others a world away too.

So be kind to others you encounter. Those gestures will impact the those you're directly connected to. And then that vibe will spread across the planet. It's an inescapable mutuality.

# -22-
# Finding Nemo

In her book *The Profit of Kindness: How to Influence Others, Establish Trust, and Build Lasting Business Relationships*, international speaker Jill Lublin shares:

"When you decide to get into business, you begin swimming with the sharks. Therefore, every business decision, idea, innovation, and communication is based on staying alive in those infested waters. Except I don't agree. My version of doing good business looks less like bloody, shark-infested waters and more like a Finding Nemo movie where all species come together, making for a magical, harmonious, colorful, fun experience, and always with a great lesson at the end."

Lublin goes on to make the point that good business is really about creating friendships that are uplifting and encouraging. It doesn't mean that there aren't bad days. It simply means that when you encounter them there are people there to pull you through – because you've done the same for them.

# -23-
## It Starts With You

According to the book *Power Networking: 55 Secrets of Personal & Professional Success* by Donna Fisher and Sandy Vilas:

"The first step in becoming a powerful networker is to get your own life in order. Orient your life around the values and principles that are important to you – those qualities that are the core of life for you, those that make your life worthwhile and give it meaning and satisfaction."

As they elaborate, if surrounding yourself with people of high character and reliability is important, then it's vital that you be of good character and reliable. The reality is that you tend to attract into your life people who are like you. So, whatever you commit to – honesty … compassion … good health … whatever – those are the people who will fill in around you.

So, become the person you want to associate with.

## -24-
## 15 Lies

Go tell a fib. Go ahead. Conflate one simple thing to improve the facts or enhance how you look. No big deal, right? But to support that tiny falsehood, you'll need to manufacture other lies to support it. Some estimate that it takes an additional 15 lies to cover up an initial one.

That's not good. But it's not horrible either. With a little effort, you can sort through how these 15 supporting lies sound – and feel. No problem, right? But wait a minute. You'll need additional supporting lies to shore up the 15 supporting lies. Working a calculator: 15 times 15 is 225.

Whoa! That's a lot. It feels as if you'll need a whole playbook to cover up one small, white lie.

Do you know what's easy? The truth. Okay, it might be unflattering. But others will respect that. And from this honesty they will come to know, like and trust you. So in the end, the truth will serve you better.

# -25-
# Stop the Conversation

According to research conducted at Harvard University, more often than not, small talk conversations go on longer than one or both participants would like. Now, this study does not suggest that you eliminate small talk from your networking routine. Rather, the takeaway is that you just need to be a little more prudent as to who you might talk to and for how long.

The logic is relatively straightforward: If you get out of the conversation you don't want to have sooner, you could spend more time in ones that you do want to have. So, when you sense that a conversation has run its course, don't be afraid to politely excuse yourself from it.

This is the reality. If there is going to be an ongoing relationship, you will talk to that person again later. But if it's unlikely there will be a relationship, then cutting a conversation short is the prudent thing to do.

## -26-
## It's Not About You

On his Daily Shake Up video message, leadership coach Jeff Nischwitz (Nish-wits) shared:

"Yes, you have objectives and it's not about you.

"Yes, you have responsibilities and it's not about you.

"Yes, you'll often get the credit for successes and it's not about you.

"Yes, you'll often be the one up front, center stage and the voice of the organization or team and it's not about you.

"Yes, people will report to you and it's not about you.

"Yes, you'll likely be held responsible when things go wrong and it's still not about you."

As Nischwitz goes on to share, leadership is about serving others – just as being a responsible networking partner is about serving others. And once you lean into this notion – and look for opportunities to serve others rather than be served – you will enhance your ability to influence others. Moreover, others will want to be around you.

# -27-
# The Future Is Completely Open

In her book *The Magical Guide To Bliss*, inspirational speaker and success coach Meg Nocero encourages you to let go of the past. In so doing, she declares "The future is completely open. As long as you live and breathe, you have time to write the best chapters of your life. Today is a new day in your journey; unwritten chapters await you."

Nocero offers an exciting insight. There is nothing that prevents you from starting anew. There is nothing to say that you can't go back to school, embark on a new career adventure, or live whatever dream you have for yourself. You are not too old. It's never too late. And there are no rules as to how your future must be.

Yes, you need to take lessons from the past. But other than that, leave behind whatever baggage that was associated with it. Then declare that you're embarking on a whole new life.

# -28-
# Making a Difference

This story has made the rounds on social media a time or two … likely much more … but it's worth repeating.  It goes …

An old man walked on a shore littered with thousands of starfish - beached and dying after a storm.  As he did, he noticed a young girl picking them up and flinging them back into the ocean.

"Why do you bother?"  The old man scoffed.  "You're not saving enough to make a difference."

The young girl picked up another starfish and sent it spinning back to the water.  "Made a difference to that one," she said.

Never underestimate the power and impact of the small things you do. Smiling at a stranger. Holding a door open for someone. Offering an unsolicited compliment. While none may actually change the world, every act changes the world for someone.

## -29-
## Best Laid Plans Gone Awry

Networking thought-leader Matt Ward shared in his book *MORE* a quote from Scottish poet Robert Burns: "The best-laid plans of mice and men sometimes go awry." Ward goes on to explain that just as the efforts of the hard-working mouse were destroyed by a farmer, life doesn't always go as planned.

Ward, however, encourages you to use this to your advantage. He explains that if you have rough patches in your life, then so do people in your network. Low sales. Lost of a client or key employee. Technology setbacks. Whatever.

Use these moments as opportunities to help your network. Ward remarks, "Be present and available to listen – really listen – and remind them it won't always be like this. Go out of your way to show your care and concern."

Ward is right. While this effort might seem simple and small to you, for the person you're reaching out to it could turn their entire day around.

# -30-
# Vision Of Possibilities

Mark Given, author and innovator of the trust-based philosophy, made the point in one of his weekly newsletters that every great endeavor started with a vision.

He shared: "Sculptors see potential in a stone; builders begin with a design on a blueprint; students see their name on a diploma; Olympic athletes visualize themselves on a podium. Throughout time...the art of the possible has built cities, technologies, and leaders we admire." Given's words beg the question: What's the big vision you have for yourself?

Everyone's life is metaphorically a giant slab of granite. It's up to you to sculpt it into something wonderful. But that creation won't just happen. You need to work to carve, chisel and hone. But before any of that, you need to have a sense as to what the end product looks like.

This is vision. And as Given indicates, if you wanted something great from your life, you need one.

# -31-
# Bend Like a Palm

In her book *The Magical Guide To Bliss*, Meg Nocero, encourages you in the midst of change to follow your intuition and "Learn to bend like a palm," so you don't end up "breaking like an oak in a heavy storm."

The storms of change are all around. And they come in all shapes and sizes, especially in times of technology and globalization. And often those changes don't always work in your favor. That's life. And you can't control it.

But what is in your control is how you deal with change. Sure, there are moments where the change is unjust, and you need to resist it. Outside of these moments, however, you need to be flexible.

You must learn to give into the change. You must learn to lean out of the way of change. You must learn to bend like a palm.

## -32-
## Endless Aspects of Networking

In Germain Moody's book *The 40 Laws of Networking: Keys For Creating Global Influence, Wealth, and Power* he shares, "There are endless networking opportunities awaiting us every single day … in a cab … at work … at the gym or at a party … at church … in traffic … on an airplane. Wherever the opportunity presents itself you should network."

Moody is right. Networking is about relationships. And relationships involve people. And people are all around you. And most of them are waiting for you ignite a conversation. Something like:

So how is your day going?

That's a wonderful tie. Where did you get it?

I couldn't help but notice your accent. Where are you from?

As Moody goes on to share by embracing this openness to networking you "formulate an atmosphere to become rich in all aspects. Not just money, but also rich in joy, health, family, friends, and the desire within to help others succeed."

# -33-
# Good In Bad Days

Michael Roderick, host of *The Access to Anyone* podcast, shared in his Investing In People newsletter that he's come to learn that bad days bestow upon you a powerful gift – empathy.

Roderick shares, "When we have a bad day, we experience the pain and frustration of that day firsthand. Because we experience it we now have a much clearer picture of what it feels like to be in that place, what language describes it, and what someone in that position might think."

He goes on to explain that bad days are not just learning experiences for you personally. They are also an opportunity to learn about the experiences of others.

So, when you have a setback or failure, remember that others endure those too. And in those moments remember well the feeling. From that you'll have gleaned some good from that bad day.

# -34-
## Take Care of Your Body

From time to time, British billionaire businessman and adventurer Sir Richard Branson is asked to share his best piece of business advice. His response is not "Work hard." Nor is it "Build a great team around you." And it's not "Have a clear vision as to where you're going."

While Branson would likely encourage each of these, his best piece of business advice is consistently this: Exercise. He goes on to explain that "if you don't take care of yourself, you can't take care of your business."

Business ... whether you're a corporate CEO, solopreneur, or somewhere in between ... is hard work, long hours, and often high stress. As such, you need to be healthy. Exercise is key to that.

And this routine can be simple. Take brisket walks a few times a week. Do some light lifting as well as work on your core and flexibility. Take care of your body and your body will take care of you.

## -35-
## The Glass Is Always Full

In his blog *What If: Reflections on Leadership, Life and Technology*, marketing expert Chris Spanier shares that he is an optimist at heart and illustrated it by saying "I once joked with a friend that the glass isn't just half full but that you get 'half a cup of air, too!'"

Spanier reminds that you shouldn't let yourself fall into a delusional state or deny reality. But with time and perspective you can find good in most anything. And why is that important you might ask? Well, it's really simple. As Spanier shares, "if deliberately look for the positive around you, you will find it … if only because you've told yourself to look."

In short, an optimistic mindset tends to create a self-fulfilling prophecy. So, the glass is neither half full nor half empty. Rather, it's always full.

## -36-
## The Two Travelers and The Farmer

Here's a quick story: A traveler came upon a farmer hoeing in his field. He asked: "What sort of people live in the next town?" The farmer replied, "What were they like where you've come from?"

"They were a bad lot. Troublemakers. Lazy too. Incredibly selfish. None could be trusted. I'm happy to be moving on." The farmer replied, "Well, I'm afraid that you'll find the same sort in the next town." Disappointed, the traveler trudged on.

Later, another traveler came along and also asked, "What sort of people live in the next town?" Again, the farmer replied, "What were the people like where you've come from?"

"They were the best people in the world. Hard working, honest, and friendly. I'm sorry to leave." The farmer replied, "You'll find the same sort in the next town."

The lesson: What you see in the world you'll always seem to find.

# -37-
# Intelligence Is Overrated

In his April 2012 *Forbes* article titled, Intelligence is Overrated: What You Really Need To Succeed, Keld Jensen reveals that experts estimate that only 15 percent of your financial success comes from your knowledge and skills. That is, all that time and effort learning your craft and building experience accounts for a relatively small percentage of your success.

What's accounts for the remaining 85%? Simple: Your ability to connect with other people. It's true. It's not what you know. It's not even who you know. Rather the overwhelming majority of your success comes down to how you interact with others.

So next time you sit down with a colleague or client, before you jump into a conversation about business strategy or the technical ins and outs of your industry, ask how they're doing. Genuinely listen. Care about what they say. Make it important to your ongoing relationship. That will drive great success.

## -38-
## Cows Don't Give Milk

One day, a dairy farmer gathered his children around and said, "This is the secret of life: Cows don't give milk."

His children giggled and then quickly challenged: "Yes, they do. We see it every day."

The farmer clarified. "I know what you see. But the cow doesn't give milk. We get up at 4 a.m., go to the barn, tie the tail, hobble the legs of the cow, sit on the stool, and do the work. That is the secret of life, the cow does not give milk. You milk her or you don't get milk."

The farmer makes an important distinction. Success in life is not a matter of wishing, asking, and obtaining. Success is about knowing what you want and then undertaking the necessary actions to make it happen.

## -39-
## A Big, Small Thing

Generally, no one fails on the big things. It's the little things, however, that trips them up. For example, few people forget to pay the mortgage. However, they might slip up on that annual magazine subscription.

The same is true with networking events. You remember to show up, right? And you've got your business cards too. Moreover, you're sure that you look the professional part. But you might not be so great with names.

Now, this seems like such a small thing. But it's not. You see, when you take the time to remember someone's name, you indicate that you value the connection with them. Moreover, when you endeavor to pronounce their name correctly, you subtly imply the person's importance.

In short, these simple acts are big, small things that serve to make others feel significant in your world. And these big, small things endear them to you.

## -40-
## Tread Into New Waters

In his book *The 40 Laws of Networking: Keys for Creating Global Influence, Wealth and Power*, Germaine Moody reminds that "Networking is not just to connect with those of like passions and interests. Networking is for treading into new waters, discovering fresh ideas, possessing new lands, and experiencing the unlimited."

Moody is inspiring. There are seven billion people on this planet. And they come in all varieties. You should connect with as much of that diversity as you can. In so doing, you will learn from unique perspectives and talents. You can learn to appreciate the differences. And revel in all the things you have in common.

To make this happen, grab coffee, or hop on a call with someone you hardly know. Or perhaps attend a seminar or an event that is outside of the mainstream for your industry or profession. In short, as Moody suggestions, find opportunities to tread into new waters.

## -41-
## Filler Or Dipper

In her book, *The Profit of Kindness: How to Influence Others, Establish Trust, and Build Lasting Business Relationships*, international speaker Jill Lublin shares an insight she learned from the grandfather of positive psychology – Donald Clifton.

Lublin explains that metaphorically everyone has a bucket and your interactions with them either fills it with positive vibes or dip energy from it. Obviously, being a filler is more advantageous that being a dipper.

She goes on to explains that you can be a filler by simply not focusing on what's wrong, but rather what's right. What are the good things that others do and say? What value do they bring to the situation? Then let them know how you feel.

When you do that, you find opportunities to notice positive things and share your gratitude for them. This serves to fill their bucket with positive emotions and builds your relationship with them.

# -42-
# The Seeds of Altruism

Networking is about adding value to others. Giving referrals. Making introductions. Sharing information and opportunities. Being encouraging. It's truly a mindset of generosity. And once you achieve this mindset, all these wonderful things start happening for you.

This generous mindset germinates from the seeds of altruism. And this is nothing more than thinking about others. Thinking with respect to everyone you meet, "How can I add a little extra happiness to this person's world?" Thinking with respect to every situation you come upon, "How can I make this better in some way?"

Then when you happen upon answers to these questions – whether it's simply holding a door open or parking further from the door – swing into action.

If you focus on being thoughtful toward others and then acting upon it, eventually your thoughtfulness becomes a habit. Then soon your adding real value to the world. And then real value will come back to you.

## -43-
## Become Formidable

A single wall is not a sturdy structure. Push on it and it feels as if a stiff breeze could easily topple it. But when you add a second wall, the two shore one another up. Add a third, even better ... and so on. That's what made forts and castles so impenetrable throughout history. The series of connecting walls bolstered the strength of the entire structure.

Relate this to life. You, yourself, are but a single wall. You alone are not meaningless, but it's not a sturdy exist either. A single challenge can send you reeling.

But when you add someone to your world, that relationship supports you. And you support it back. Add a third person to your existence and life gets even better. But don't stop there. Build a figurative fort of great relationships in your life. They will make you more formidable in your pursuit of success.

# -44-
# Who Would You Like To Meet?

Often the most valuable thing you have to offer those in your network is your network itself. In other words, an introduction to someone else can provide lasting, almost-immeasurable benefits.

When you introduce people within your network to others, you literally set in motion a lifetime of new contacts, a wealth of information and gateways to thousands of dollars of opportunities. Career. Business. Life. As long as you have two people in your network who don't know each other, you have value to share.

And as such, when you meet someone new, while that person might not hold any value for you, that person represents value that you can share with other people you know.

So, to serve your networking best, the most important question you should ask is: Who are the types of people you'd like to meet?

# -45-
# What If ...

What if you knew that every time you smiled, you'd added a few minutes to your life? What if every time you did something kind, you added an hour to your life? What you if did something generous, the good Lord extended your time on the planet by an extra day?

Granted, even in this day and age, we don't know for sure what acts of benevolence – whether planned or complete random – do to human longevity. But speculating can be fun. And answering that question can serve to give meaning and focus to a scientific mind.

But, while no one can say for sure whether a simple smile, human kindness, or wonderful generosity will extent your life, we do know this for sure. These actions will serve to increase your enjoyment of whatever life you have left. And that is reason enough to embark on a life of generosity.

## -46-
## 7 Steps To Great First Impressions

Time and again, studies show that within mere fractions of a second, people are forming judgements about you. These opinions encompass your level of competence, sincerity, trustworthiness and much more. All within a blink of an eye.

So, you want to nail that first impression, especially when the stakes are high, such as in a job interview or meeting prospective clients.

David Shriner-Cahn, host of *Smashing the Plateau* podcast and consultant to those migrating from the corporate to the solo consulting worlds, offers these seven tips.

Number one, smile and, number two, make eye contact. Number three, do your home in advance, so that, number four, you ask insightful questions with this new person. And number five, once you've asked those insightful questions, engage in active listening. As you do, number six, exhibit positive body language. The key to all of this is number seven: practice, practice, practice.

# -47-
# No Cold Sales

No doubt, you're familiar with the notion of a cold calling. You know. The practice of picking up the phone. Dialing a complete stranger. Totally interrupting their world. All to tell someone you don't even know that what you've got is exactly what they need. And that you're only calling because you really, really care.

Of course, now technology also allows for electronic versions of this very sterile outreach – e-mail merges, automated texts, and messaging bots. But while – sadly – cold calling is still very much a thing, what has never really existed is the cold sale.

However, you choose initiate business – cold call, warm outreach, or red-hot referral – before the transaction will happen there must be some semblance of a relationship.

So, as you need people to know, like and trust you before they will do business with you, you should try to build that relationship as soon as possible.

## -48-
## Just One Plate

American comedian Tom Hanks once remarked, "Eating everything you want is not that much fun. When you live a life with no boundaries, there's less joy. If you can eat anything you want to, what's the fun in eating anything you want to?"

Hanks certainly meant his statement as a metaphor. You can't have everything in life. Nor do you want it all. There is something to the notion of working hard for things. And then being successful with some of those endeavors. And not so much with others.

It's the longing for the things you don't have that makes the ultimate success that much more gratifying. Even the occasional failures sweeten the feeling of accomplishment.

Following on with Hanks' metaphor, success in life is a buffet. But like a buffet, you don't get it all. Rather, you simply get a single plate. And you need to work hard to load stuff on to it.

## -49-
## I Quit

In the introduction of her book *The Magical Guide To Bliss*, Meg Nocero, shares a powerful mission statement that everyone can embrace in one form or another. And it's born out of just two words: "I Quit."

I QUIT!

I QUIT a place where I am no longer able to develop my talent.

I QUIT fear and wasting my time on things that no longer deserve my worth.

I QUIT seeking and needing approval from others to define my worth.

I QUIT beating myself up mentally and sabotaging my own peace and freedom.

I QUIT not loving and believing in myself and my purpose.

I QUIT not paying attention to the signs that show me the way.

I QUIT and SURRENDER to love and bliss!

Quitting is often considered a bad thing. However, Nocero's quitting marks the first step on the road to success. With that, what are you going to have the courage to quit?

## -50-
## Networking of the Gods

Scott Mason, transformational coach, and host of the *Purpose Highway* podcast shared this insight:

"The king of the gods, Zeus, wanted to set up a whole new world order to build Olympus. But he was smart enough to understand that the prior gods, the Titians, were simply too strong for him to fight on his own. So, in order to bring about change, he gathered an army. Goddesses of wisdom. Ironworkers. Creatures with magical powers. They worked together and the Titians fell."

Mason is right. If you want to build your own Olympus ... however you define it ... you need to gather people around you.

The idea that you can do anything alone is, as Mason puts it, a toxic myth. Zeus recognized this. The Titans didn't and lost in a big way. So double down on building a network of special people to help create your world.

## -51-
## Complain, Blame, Excuses

In her book *The Radical Empowerment Method*, professional speaker, and personal coach Carrie Verrocchio shares that you "always have the opportunity to choose to be empowered or choose to stay mired in complaining, blaming, and excuse making."

But Verrocchio goes on to encourage you to not choose these negative behaviors, citing three reasons. One, it doesn't help. Not at all. In fact, the trifecta of 'complain, blame and excuses' simply takes time and energy from making things better.

Second, engaging in these behaviors wires your brain for negativity. And with that, you simply attract more negativity into your life. And finally, no one likes to be around someone who is mired in complaining, blaming and excuse making. So, these behaviors drive people away.

Moreover, these are each exhausting – emotionally and mentally. So, if you feel yourself wanting to complain, blame or make an excuse, catch yourself and re-route your thinking.

# -52-
# The Tapestry of Success

The next time you hear someone else dismissing the problem of another as "not concerning them," remind them that everyone is a vital thread in the tapestry of success. Think about it.

There are seven billion people on this big blue rock circling the sun. And somehow, everyone is connected. So, you're part of this network. We all are.

Now, when one of person succeeds, it makes the world a better place. Then, in time, that goodness works its way over to you. Likewise, when one person is hurting or threatened, you're eventually at risk, too.

So, when you see someone needing assistance, help them. Even if you don't think it matters to you, it somehow does.

## -53-
## The Count Doesn't Count

Social media is great. LinkedIn. Facebook. Twitter. Instagram. And the list of platforms grows.

On any of these, you can communicate and engage with others on the things that matter to you. These enable you to reconnect with friends and family where time might have distanced your relationship. And these allow you to build acquaintances with those you might never have a chance to meet ... across town ... cross country ... and even around the world.

And while social media can be empowering, don't get caught up tracking the numbers of connections. Or watching your followers grow. Or become mesmerized by the tallies of likes and comments.

Rather the true power of social media is the actual friends you can build through it. You know, those trusting bonds with another that you call upon when you need it most. In short, yes, you can count the numbers, but it's the relationships that really count.

# -54-
# Mess To Message

Peter Biadasz, President of Total Publishing and Media and author of *Write Your First Book* and 17 others, has a mantra. "From the mess comes the message."

Biadasz goes on to elaborate that 'things' happen in your life that are somewhat less than favorable. And from time to time, you make missteps. But in any of these unfortunate moments there is a message or a lesson from which you can learn and grow.

For example, you lose a client or not get that promotion. Those situations are never fun. But if in that moment you stop. Take a deep breath. And take the time to reflect on how you can be better or do better. If you're honest with yourself, there is a take-away. Something that will help you ensure that the next time you are successful.

Sure, no one likes the pain of failure or chaos. But the mess always leads to a message.

# -55-
# The Steady

Author Mark Given, innovator of the trust-based philosophy, remarked in his weekly newsletter that there are two types of habits: Good and Bad.

With that, he shared, "The compound effect of your habits over time will either work for you or against you. It was the tortoise not the hare that won the race. But slow did not create the win, it was the steady. Good habits are the steady. When implemented consciously and consistently, they help us win."

As Given alludes, creating positive habits of resilience and determination are key to success no matter what path you choose to race down or who you seek to race against. There will be good days and there will be bad. There will be days of progress and days of setback.

But none of that matters in the end, as long as you commit to the 'steady.' Slowly plotting towards where you want to be.

## -56-
## X's and O's; Sally's and Joe's

Many see networking as this very mechanical activity. Tactics. Strategies. Executing on a playbook, if you will. Methodically carrying out activities much like a sports team executes on a game plan. Show up. Be punctual. Stand here. Do this. Say that. If you checked all the boxes, then, you can't miss.

But it's not like that all. Networking is about people. It's about relationships. It's about handshakes, hugs, and pats on the back. It's about listening, caring about others, and taking actions that benefit them.

Sure, you need to show up. And, yes, you need to be on time. And be present. Those are a given. And, likewise, you need do and say certain things. But it's not one size-fits-all. What you do and what you say changes depending upon the moment. And the person you are interacting with.

Networking is not about X's and O's. Rather it's about Sally's and Joe's.

## -57-
## Do the Next Right Thing

Chances are, you've heard the phrase, "do the right thing." And likely, you do. When confronted with a decision to act in one particular way or another, you choose to do what is just, fair, and in the best interest of the greater good of the situation. Simple concept, right?

A way to up the ante on this notion, however, is to commit to, "do the next right thing." That is, don't wait for that moment to benefit the greater good, but rather seek out these moments.

This advocates taking an active approach to serving the world around you. In short, take the initiative to find the person or situation that could use assistance. Then acting upon that opportunity. Lending a hand. Making an introduction. Being encouraging or supportive.

In short, doing the 'next' right thing is a step up from simply just doing the right thing.

# -58-
# Stepping Into Your PowPow Shoes

In her book *The Radical Empowerment Method*, professional speaker and personal coach Carrie Verrocchio introduces the term "stepping into your PowPow shoes."

She shares, "Stepping into your PowPow shoes is stepping into your confidence, your radiance, your best, brilliant self. Being unapologetically YOU. Saying yes when you mean yes and no when you mean no. Stepping into your PowPow shoes means learning to laugh and find joy – even when life is hard. Especially when life is hard."

Sure, Verrocchio's notion of PowPow shoes might make you smile, but it should make you think too. What is it that empowers you to believe in dreams and declare that you have value to share with the world?

It might be a vision in your mind, a song, a mantra, a series of affirmations, or all of the above. Whatever it is, put on those PowPow shoes and venture forth.

## -59-
## Compromises and Constraints

You can't have your cake and eat it too. You can't have great rates of return on your investments without being subject to a comparable degree of risk. And you can't have a low auto insurance premium with top shelf coverages.

Life is full of compromises and constraints. You simply cannot have it all. And this is true of most anything, including success.

Success takes commitment. You need to dedicate yourself to something, whatever that might be. And then you need to hone your knowledge, skills, and talents according. You won't find success focused on something today and then something else tomorrow.

Success takes hard work. Sure, balance is important. Resting and recharging is a necessity. But you won't achieve lasting success if you don't put in the necessary toil.

So, if you truly want success, you need to eliminate the constraints on your efforts and make no compromises on your commitment.

# -60-
# Treasure Map

You're likely familiar with the notion of a treasure map — markings, usually on paper or parchment, that detail the location of some object of value. Gold. Jewels. Or artifacts.

But here is the thing, the value of a treasure map is not wrapped up in the object itself. As long as there is valuable treasure out there, the map is worth far, far more than the paper it's written on.

Metaphorically speaking, the people in your network are like treasure maps. Sure, they themselves have a certainly value to them — perhaps as a client. But their true value is wrapped up in what they can lead you to. Other connections. Useful information. And insight on important opportunities.

But, unlike an aged map leading fixed riches, the value your network to grows. Think about it. Every new connection is another treasure map, leading to more connections. And thus, the riches are endless.

## -61-
## Be Open or Selective?

You want to add great people to your network, right?
Everyone does. Some might argue that you simply need to
be more selective. Actually, however, the opposite is true.
For example, you determine that by being selective, for
every four people you meet, one turns into a great, long-
term professional relationship. That sounds great. One in
four. Twenty-five percent.

But it sounds less impressive, however, if you only met
four people over the course of a year. What might it look
like being more open to meeting whomever?

Continuing with the above example, what if only ten
percent of the people you meet turned into great
relationships? But at the same time, you increased the
number of people you meet ten-fold – going from four to
40? Work the math. You'd have a four-fold increase in
valued relationships.

Now, what leads to a better result – being open or being
selective?

# -62-
# Gratitude Bookends

In her book *The Radical Empowerment Method*, professional speaker and personal coach Carrie Verrocchio encourages: "Bookend your days with gratitude" She challenges you to start the day and end the day jotting down the things you have to be grateful for.

And she goes on to add that if you get stuck, she offers a plethora of suggestions. "You have a journal or a piece of paper. You're holding a pen. You have coffee or tea to start the day. A job, business, or the pursuit of education in the middle. And you can read or write. And you likely end the day in a bed, with clean sheets and a decent pillow."

Verrocchio shares that "The list of things to be grateful for is endless." Moreover, she explains that being grateful improves your mindset, your brain health, and your overall health. It makes you more productive. It makes you happier and improves your self-esteem. And that alone is something to be grateful for.

## -63-
## Learn From Charlie Brown's Teacher

Do you remember the Charlie Brown cartoons? Linus. Lucy. Peppermint Patty. Schroeder. And, of course, Snoopy. Then there was Charlie Brown's teacher – Mrs. Donovan. Remember her? What did she say? "Wah, wah, wah, wah."

Essentially what the teacher said was so rote that it defied description. Sadly, many people are the same way when it comes to introducing themselves. It's the same thing, over and over. In time it sounds just like, "Wah, wah, wah, wah."

Don't be like Charlie Brown's teacher. Have a little variety in your how you introduce yourself. In short, do not limit yourself to a single 30-second commercial. Develop one for colleagues. Develop one for vendors. Develop one for competitors. Develop one for each aspect of your business. Create an entire menu of introductions.

In short, make what you have to say memorable to others.

## -64-
## Double Down on Giving

There is a notion in the world of building professional relationships that you need to give to get. That is, add value to the world around you and opportunities will come back to you. You know, the sort of stuff you need to advance your life. And do you know what? It's absolutely true. What you do for others comes back to you in time.

With that, you can approach life by giving a bit and waiting for that moment or indication that something comes back to you. And then, and only then, do you give again.

Or you can double down on the notion of give to get. Completely surrender to it. Add value whenever you can. Give referrals. Share information. Make introductions. Volunteer. Mentor. Be encouraging and so on. Do these things and never look back trying to size up or sort out how it's working. Simply trust the process.

## -65-
## Celebrate the Try

Failures. Setbacks. And Disappointments. None of them are fun. Actually, they all stink. No one likes to come up short.

But, that said, these are not so horrible either. Really! Sure, a failure can feeling defeating ... a setback indicates ground you need to recapture ... and disappointments can downright hurt. But you don't encounter any of these unless you're pushing yourself and trying to achieve something you haven't done before.

This is the reality. Not everyone can write a New York Times bestseller. Not everyone is able run a sub-four-hour marathon (or complete a marathon at all). Not everyone builds a business into the next Fortune 500 wonder.

The fact that you might try to do anything equally audacious, however, places you the top one percent of people on the entire planet. So don't lament what you haven't been able to do. Rather, celebrate the things you tried.

## -66-
## Jargon Sucks!

Jargon sucks! It does. It sucks. No, not in the sense of the definition meaning bad. Rather, jargon, quite literally, sucks business out of your hands.

No doubt you know your craft well. But outside of your professional inner circle, few people really understand it and they certainly aren't hip to the special words or expressions you might use to talk about things.

So, while you might sound smart firing out terminology ... like, decree ... 203K ... RMDs ... FASB ... or fisbo ... this verbiage actually causes eyes to glaze over with confusion. And when uncertainty reigns supreme, you better believe it's costing you in terms of clients, referrals, and other measures of cold hard cash.

Yes, technical lingo is an important verbal shorthand for your industry. You're best to use it there. But beyond that, jargon sucks. So, in general conversations use language everyone can understand.

# -67-
# Facts and Opinions

The earth is round. It revolves around the sun. These are well-established, scientific facts. And there is no credible evidence otherwise.

The sun setting over an open body of water is a romantic event. This is mere an opinion. Facts and opinions. It's important to know the difference. You're welcome to challenge a factual assertion of another. Sure, be respectful in your approach. But, nevertheless, a quick search of the Internet should settle that discussion.

Someone's opinion, however, is a different matter. That viewpoint has been formed based on their unique experience. Accept that.

Sure, you can have a different opinion. And you're welcome to respectfully share it. But it's simply pointless to argue with their view of whatever – the state of business, who's the best team or the relative beauty of a sunset. It's their opinion. Respect that.

# -68-
# Habitually Complimentary

In her book *Dare To Connect*, Susan Jeffers reminds us that "the purpose of a compliment is not to make others like you, but rather to enrich their lives in some way." In short, complimenting others is altruistic. Knowing this, it's important to make complimenting others part of your routine.

In her book *Nonstop Networking*, Andrea Nierenberg offers a suggestion for becoming habitually complimentary. She recommends that until you get in the habit of giving daily compliments that you start each day with five pennies in your right pocket.

Then each time you give a compliment or offer up some genuine praise, you simply shift one penny from your right pocket to your left. Obviously, the objective is to end the day with all five pennies in your left pocket.

Through this strategy you will consistently focus on finding opportunities to compliment others. And this insight is more than just someone's two cents.

## -69-
## Better Than Yesterday

You can't be better than anyone. Think about it. The world is too complicated. You might best someone at a particular aspect of life or business, but then they'd likely trump you on something else. So, you can't be better than anyone.

And if you endeavor to play the "I'm better" game, you'll find yourself on a never-ending treadmill of one-upmanship. And that takes the fun out of life long-term.

No, you can't be better than anyone. But you can look to continually improve. In life, if there is any long-term competition at all, that's it. You looking to outdo the person you were the day before.

As best-selling author Dr. Adam Grant shares, "Striving to be better shifts the focus from victory to mastery. You're competing with your past self and raising the bar for your future self."

So, don't look to be better than anyone. Just strive to be better than yesterday.

## -70-
## Creating An Invisible Web

In his book *The 40 Laws of Networking*, social architect Germaine Moody shares a quote from a magician living near Malta. The person shares:

"Networking is important because eventually you create a web of potential leads that in turn create work and prosperity for both yourself and a number of other people within your network. You will also have several opportunities to increase your brand or visibility through the many other networks, people in your network are affiliated with."

This Malta magician is right. The invisible tethers between the people you know and the people they know creates a web that you can tap into for business, referrals, introductions, information, and a variety of opportunities. And the more people you know, the wider that net becomes. And the better you know the people around you, the stronger the bonds.

So, networking involves building relationships with others, but it's really about creating this invisible web you can benefit from.

# -71-
## Sewn Into History

Many people view networking as having its advent in the later decades of the 20th century – born out of the post-industrial revolution where society moved into a service-based economy.

The reality is this: Networking is nothing more than relationships. Relationships that offer mutual benefits. Relationships that provide for the overall improvement of humanity. As such, networking has guided the human race for eons. And examples of it litter history.

Consider Betsy Ross – a seamstress born into a family decisively against violence. So, when she fell in love with and married a man who was staunchly behind the Revolutionary War, Ross found herself disowned.

But this marriage connected her to a new religion. One where she sat by George Washington at church services each week. As such our first President didn't need to look far for someone to create American flag.  So, you could say networking is sewn into history.

## -72-
## Greyhounds Versus a Cheetah

In the United Kingdom in the 1930s, an experiment was conducted to see if greyhounds could compete with the speed of a cheetah. When the cages were opened, however, onlookers were shocked that the cheetah didn't move. They asked the race coordinator why the cheetah didn't race.

He said, "Sometimes trying to prove that you're the best is an insult to your self-worth. There is no need to lower yourself to other people's level to make them understand your skills, qualities, and contributions. It is better to save your energy for more worthy endeavors. A cheetah uses its speed to hunt, not to prove to dogs that it is faster and stronger."

As this relates to you, don't waste your time and energy trying to prove your value to those who will never understand it. Rather lean into adding value to those who will appreciate it.

## -73-
## Epidemic Loneliness

According to a study conducted by researchers at Harvard University that spanned decades and decades, loneliness has a corrosive impact on life and society. In fact, isolation can be as unhealthy as smoking a half a pack of cigarettes a day.

The lesson is clear. Commit to having people in your life. Family. Friends. Colleagues and neighbors. Get up out of your chair and off the couch. Engage in your community. Serve. Volunteer. Share your knowledge. Mentor others.

These things keep you from being amongst the ranks of the lonely. Moreover, sharing your presence does the same for others too. And avoiding loneliness also stymies the negative aspects of it.

Sure, it's important to have "me" time, where you can quietly recharge and reflect. But that should never be all the time. You need others in your world. And others need you too.

# -74-
## Ikigai

Get your head around this term: Ikigai. **This is a** term that compounds two Japanese words: iki, meaning "alive," and gai, meaning "what makes life worth living."

Most people associate ikigai with a diagram created in 2014 by Marc Winn, a business coach and entrepreneur from a small island nation of Guernsey. Winn encourages you to draw four circles that overlap with each other.

Then you label each circle based on what it represents. One, represents what you love to do. The next is what you're good at. The third is what world needs. And the final one is what you can be paid for.

The place where all these circles overlap represents your ikigai. Whatever that activity is, is where you're most alive, most able to contribute to the world, most beneficial to the world, and yet able to sustain a life worth living. Think on this. Find your ikigai.

Frank Agin

## -75-
## Generational Capabilities

Generational wealth: The notion of passing valuable assets from one generation to the next, then the next. Sounds alluring, huh? It has the feel of royalty or industry barons.

This is problematic, however. Future generations grow exponentially – children, grandchildren, and on. Quickly, the lineage outpaces the growth of assets. Additionally, descendants don't appreciate what it took to build the fortune. Thus, in time, wealth is squandered. So, passing on wealth is difficult.

But do you know what's not difficult to pass on? Capabilities. Think about it. There are so many capabilities you can easily pass on to the next generation.

A positive attitude. A resilient mindset. Skills and talents. A tireless work ethic. A sense of discipline. Insight, knowledge, and a love of learning. Kindness, compassion, and empathy.

Create generational capabilities. Those inspirations will never deplete. Moreover, the generations that come after you will eagerly pass them on.

# -76-
# Where's the Beef

In a 1984 commercial, a trio of woman examined a skimpy fast-food hamburger. At a point, one woman cried out, "Where's the beef?" This instantly became a slogan for Wendy's Hamburgers, as well as a catchphrase for underdelivering.

R. David Thomas, the founder of Wendy's Hamburgers, was an unlikely success. As a high school dropout, he was to be best suited to be just a fast-food worker as opposed to a fast-food tycoon.

But when he came up with the idea for Wendy's — one of America's largest hamburger chains — he executed upon a great networking strategy. Rather than beating down doors for new connections to get started, he tapped into the ones he'd made over the years working his way up at Kentucky Fried Chicken.

So, where's the beef? In a networking sense, it means trying to connect with new people to accomplish something when your existing network could do it for you.

# -77-
# Networking Is Chaos

How networking works and how you'd hope it would, are two different things. You want a coordinated arrangement where you do X and then Y happens for you, as if it were a single strand of string laid out on the floor like a timeline.

But how networking works is a whole lot less tidy. After all, networking is about relationships. And relationship depend on people. And people are different. And all the circumstances they are coming from and situations they are going to have a seemingly endless number of variables.

For that reason, networking tends to feel like chaos. It's like a tangled wad of yarn - you can't see what is connected to where.

But be patient. Allow the relationships in your life to unravel themselves. You will find, that in time, from that chaos comes order. And ultimately, you'll discover that the wad of yarn leads to exactly where you want to be.

## -78-
## Fishin' For Others

It's true. The best way to get opportunities from your network – such as, contacts, information, and opportunities – is to provide opportunities to it first. Now finding opportunities for others is like fishing. Basically, it involves three steps: Bait. Cast. And reel in the catch.

In the networking world, baiting involves learn about the unique features of your network's offerings that could be potentially beneficial or attractive to others.

Casting the hook involves casually and occasionally talking about those features with individuals who might find them attractive or beneficial.

And, then reeling in the catch is simply a matter of connecting those who have the need to those who have the attractive or beneficial offering.

Like fishing, not every bite results in a catch. So what? You're just fishing. Patiently bait, cast and reel again. Eventually, something will hit. But when you fish for opportunities, no catch is too small, as every opportunity is a keeper.

## -79-
## 10-Second Relationships

According to a study published in the *Journal of Experimental Psychology*, small talk improves one's feelings of belonging and positive emotions.

But here's the interesting part. This did not stem from 20 minutes of idle chit chat over a cup of coffee at some networking event. Rather, these experiment participants were simply instructed to strike up a short exchange with the barista at the coffee shop.

Literally, 10 second. Something as simple as "Hey, how are you today?" Or, "I really like your hair." Maybe just, "I cannot believe this gorgeous weather we're getting." That's it. And from this you get an improved mood, and you're immediately transform into a more social person.

But wait. There's more. From this, the next time you actually need to approach someone – where the stakes are higher – it's no big deal, as you're more comfortable connecting with anybody. And that's the big bonus to the 10-second relationship.

## -80-
## Stumbling Blocks To Steppingstone

Michael Josephson, internationally renowned champion of character, shares that "The difference between steppingstones and stumbling blocks is not in the event itself, but how you think about it and what you do after it."

The founder of the Character Counts movement, Josephson, goes on to allude that everyone endures failures and setbacks. But it's what you do with that moment that matters.

You can use it as the reason for quitting or your excuse for failing. And many people do, pointing to that stumbling block that tripped them up.

Or you can be unique. Special. You can figuratively step on that life challenge and use it as a means of inspiration to be better and do better. You can take from it a personal teachable moment.

As Josephson goes on to share, if you develop the discipline of positivity, you be both happier and more successful in the long run.

## -81-
## Connected By a Star

In his TEDx Talk out of Taipei, presenter Tom Chi shared that billions of years ago there was a massive star in our part of the galaxy. It was so massive, in fact, that just before it went super nova and exploded, its gravitational forces were able to create the heavy metal iron.

Those iron elements – and other elements from that massive star – then coalesced to help form our solar system. Those iron elements are the same ones that make up the iron on this planet, as well as the iron contained in our blood's hemoglobin.

WOW! We're all connected to that massive star from long ago. But, more importantly – no matter your race, religion, or political leaning – we're all connected to each other through those bits of iron.

So, even if you feel like you have nothing else in common with someone, you have that. And that should be enough to inspire you to be respectful and decent.

## -82-
## Quell "Small Talk" Fear

Let's face it. Some people are downright afraid of making conversation. They're afraid of not having anything meaningful to contribute. They're afraid of running out of conversation. And they're afraid of being in a conversation with someone they would rather not.

If any of this describes you, don't be afraid. First, the best thing you can contribute to a conversation is listening well. You can do that, right? From there, you can get by with simple affirming statements or gestures. And you have questions to keep them going. With those things, there is no way you'd ever run out of something to say.

As for fear of being engaged in small talk with that person you'd rather not, so what? Give them 15 minutes or so. How bad could it be? And you might be surprised where it leads.

So, quell your fear of small talk. Good always come from it.

## -83-
## Survival Of Your Vision

In his book *The School of Greatness*, Lewis Howes shares, "Greatness is really the survival of your vision across an extended timeline, based on your willingness to do whatever it takes in the face of adversity and to adopt the mindset to seize opportunity wherever it lives."

Envisioning what you want your success to look like is easy, especially in a quiet moment, early in the journey. It becomes much more difficult, however, when you're exhausted from weeks, months, and even years of effort. And, it's easy to compromise on your vision when you're confronted with obstacles or you experience setbacks.

As Howes implies, these are the critical moments on the path to greatness. It's at these points, when doubt might be creeping into your mind, that you need to push through. You need to convince yourself that success is just beyond the horizon. In short, do whatever you can to ensure the survival of your vision.

# -84-
# The World Needs Everyone

The world needs everyone. Yes, everyone. To do all that the world requires be done to keep civilized life going it needs everyone.

The world needs dreamers. And it needs doers. It needs people with progressive views to move the world forward. And it needs conservative ones to balance the equation. It needs those who are all about love. And the world needs the daring fighter too. It needs people who make things. And it needs people who merely serve.

Simply stated, everybody matters. And if you don't believe that, imagine a life without an aspect of society. No farmers; no food. No scientists; no advancement. No sanitation workers; well, a big heaping mess.

The world cannot operate without anyone. So, respect and appreciate the everyday contribution of the people around you that you might otherwise overlook. The world needs everyone.

## -85-
## Be Self-Deprecating

Who knows you best? Your parents? A best friend? A spouse? Your kids? The truth is, the person who knows you best, is you. You know your hopes, dreams, and aspirations. You know what your passionate about. You know your strengths. And you know your shortcomings.

Now, there is nothing horrible about your shortcomings. Everyone has got them. But if you're smart, you can use them to your advantage. How? Simple. As, Charles Schulz, famed cartoonist once said: "If I were given the opportunity to present a gift to the next generation, it would be the ability for each individual to learn to laugh at himself."

What Schulz is driving at is that if you acknowledge your flaws and even go so far as to make light of them, you serve to make yourself a little more approachable and likeable. And that's a surefire formula for attracting great people and wonderful things into your life.

## -86-
## Step Into the Now

In her book *The Magical Guide To Bliss*, Meg Nocero, advises that "If you want to move forward in life, it's futile to dwell on the past. It does you no good to judge yourself over and over again for your past mistakes. The past is done. It is the present that is bursting with potential."

Nocero makes a compelling case for stepping into the now. Sure, you can learn from the past. And it's okay to acknowledge past shortcomings. But today ... today, you are a better version of yourself because of them.

So, step into the now. Chances are prior challenges will fall away. Chances are you've now got what it takes. And chances are you'll meet with success this time.

As Nocero shares, "Give love to your present dreams, give love to yourself, and go forth."

## -87-
## The Importance of Understanding

What creates a great relationship? Most would agree that whether personal or professional a great relationship require a sense of mutual love and appreciation.

However, according to the work of social psychologist Harry Reis, with the University of Rochester, there is another ingredient that society has overlooked for years. It's the simple notion of being understood. Yes, the people around you – family, friends, and colleagues – they want to be loved and appreciated. But they want you to take the time to understand them as well.

So, if you want the best possible relationships, take the time to know the hopes and dreams of those you already love and appreciate. Why do they work so hard? What is their motivation? What truly brings them joy?

Taking the time to know these things will give you a better understanding of them. But this effort will also demonstrate your commitment to the people in your world.

## -88-
## Listen and Silent

This is an interesting insight. And maybe it's just a neat coincidence. But whatever the case, it's true. The words "listen" and "silent" are spelled with the same letters.

Now, no doubt there is much about you, that you'd like to share. Some of it is very insightful. And arguably, all of it is worthwhile.

Nevertheless, the reality is that the best relationships are forged when you aren't sharing any of it. The best relationships are born out of the moments when you listen. When you're silent.

You see, when you allow the other person to get out all the things about them and when you let them share their worthwhile insight, you give of yourself. You give time. You give attention. You give them the chance to see how they might fit into your network.

So, next time you find yourself in conversation, give of yourself. Be silent. And listen.

## -89-
## JOMO

By now, most everyone is familiar with the term FOMO. Born from text messaging, it stands for the 'fear of missing out.' And it's a reference to an anxiety associated with not being at the right place, at the right time.

This angst, in reality, has been with humanity from the moment our ancestors first created the notion of community. No one wanted to miss what happened around the fire. Then, on the street corner. And, now on the latest social media app.

But over a decade ago, Anil Dash, an entrepreneur, flipped the script and coined the term JOMO – the joy of missing out. It's the advantage of being disconnected. The benefit of removing yourself from the chaos of modern society. The power of being alone in thought. It gives you time to calm from the stresses … of whatever.

Today, find a moment or two to give yourself some JOMO.

# -90-
# Making Big Talk

There is nothing like a small talk conversation to effectively embark on a new relationship. And that idle chit chat is wonderful for re-connecting with someone you already know.

But do you know what else is important? Big talk! You know those conversations where the opinions are not all in ailment. The discussions where the stakes are high. Or that talk where emotions are heighten.

Sure, you can put these moments off. But they don't go away. So, you best face up to the reality that the "big talk" must happen. And as such, you might as well commit to making the conversation constructive.

To make this happen, take a moment to remind yourself that across from you will be a person. Someone with whom you have a relationship. A relationship that took time to create, but one which can be quickly destroyed. With that, temper your tone and choose your words carefully.

## -91-
## Actions Scream

Do you want to weigh less? Build a better network? Start a business? Buy a house? Get that soul mate into your life? Any of these ... actually, all of these are great aspirations. Write them down. Share those intentions with others.

But know this. What you say is meaningless. Why? Because day in and day out, people hear – or read about – these sorts of affirmations of intent. And often the follow through on these declarations is scant at best. So, in short, words tend to ring hollow.

Do you know what isn't ignored? What makes the people around you sit up and take notice? Simple. Action. Quietly take steps to lose weight. Get out and build those relationships. Launch the business or buy that house, and then show the world what you did.

Remember, words mere whisper and no one hears them. Actions, however, scream out and say, "I'm committed."

# -92-
# Expect Greatness

Tim Shurr, corporate trainer, motivational speaker, and high-performance psychologist, shared in his book *The Power of Optimism: Attitude Training for Those Who Want More from Life*:

"People live up to the expectations you have of them — whether positive or negative. If you look for the highest good in people, they will live up to it! So make sure that you raise your expectations of yourself and your expectations of those you love."

Shurr shares a wonderful secret for creating success. If you want to achieve great things in life, then truly expect that you can make them happen. A stellar career. A business that others admire. An enviable life. Expect those things for yourself.

Likewise, if you want great achievement for the important people in your life, share with them that you believe in them and expect that wonderful things will happen for them.

## -93-
## The Behavioral Reinforcement of Thanks

Taking the time to say thanks – however you choose to do it – is simply the right thing to do. It's polite. It's respectful. And it provides you with another meaningful touch point with your network.

But taking the time to express gratitude for something that someone has said or done, also serves to set in motion powerful psychological forces. And these influences serve to provide you lasting benefits.

Think about it. When you tell someone "Thank you," you make them feel great. They cannot help but smile. It gives them a little hit of dopamine. And they associate this with you. As a result, this subtly create an intangible incentive to repeat whatever drove the gratitude. For example, send a thank you for a referral and they will likely be looking to do more.

So, if you're looking to get more to be grateful for, be sure to express gratitude for whatever you get.

# -94-
# Vision and Action

A Japanese proverb says, "Vision without action is a dream. Action without vision is a nightmare."

Is your life a dream? You ponder day and night. You think on things that you'd like to be. And you daydream about places you'd like to go. But you never do anything to make it a reality.

Or perhaps your life is a nightmare? You grind. You toil. But you don't quite know why. You don't know where you're going. And you're not even sure where you want to be.

Neither 'vision without action' nor 'action without vision' is good. So, stop dreaming long enough to act on what's going on in your head. But take a break from the action from time to time to remind yourself what it's all for and where you're going. Remember, together vision and action are an incredible formula for success.

## -95-
## No Give, Never Get

In persuasion expert Brian Ahearn's business parable book *The Influencer: Secrets to Success And Happiness*, the protagonist John Andrews remarks: "We don't give to get. But if we don't give, you're never going to get."

The implication to this is really two-fold. First, doing for others or adding value to the world is not some tactic by which you market yourself. Rather the notion of altruism is truly a mindset by which you show up best in the world. And when you do you position yourself to succeed.

But the second implication is that having a giving heart is not enough. You need to act on those feelings for the benefits to manifest themselves. It's one thing to want to be that giver but wanting and being are not the same thing.

So, without coupling a true sense of generosity with the follow through of actually doing it, there is no true give and there never will be get.

## -96-
## Trust Your Past

Tim Shurr, corporate trainer, motivational speaker, and high-performance psychologist, shared in his book The Power of Optimism: Attitude Training for Those Who Want More from Life:

"There will always be at least one stressful situation or activity hanging overhead. But if you soothingly remind yourself that life has a miraculous way of always working things out, you'll never have to waste another ounce of energy worrying. After all, how many times have you thought to yourself, 'How am I ever going to get through this? And yet, here you are alive and kicking."

Shurr is right. Life seems to a never-ending litany of challenges. But you also are equipped with an endless reserve of energies, abilities, and tactics to overcome them.

So, whatever difficulties you now face, you will be alive and kicking tomorrow. You have the tools to make it happen. Trust that. Trust yourself. Trust your past. It's proof positive that things will work out.

## -97-
## The Silence Is Everything

Sssshhh. ... Listen. ... Do you hear it? ... Don't hear anything? It's the silence. And it might feel like nothing but it's important.

You see most people have a compulsion to fill silence. They meet someone new and want to go well beyond just sharing their name. Their conversation partner pauses for a moment – even just to catch their breath – and they take that as a cue to launch into a monolog about themselves.

But the reality is that the best relationships are forged when you allow for the silence. These are the moments when you signal a willingness to listen and quietly take in what the other person shares. In so doing, you validate their importance. And when they pause you lean into the silence as if the next words out of their mouth are the six-winning numbers in the mega lottery.

So, Sssshhh. ... Listen. ... That nothing is everything.

# -98-
# Power In Dreaming

In her book *The Magical Guide To Bliss*, life coach Meg Nocero, shares: "Life's possibilities are endless. If there comes a time when you can't see any hope on the horizon, stop and take a moment to dream. When you spend time allowing your imagination to run wild, innovative ideas will come to you like burst of sunshine on a cloudy day."

Nocero gives you a powerful tool for pursuing big things. You see, even if you're not at a hopeless point, you can stop and take a moment to envision the endless possibilities for your life.

Get in the habit of periodically just stopping what you're doing. Sit quietly. Or take a short stroll. Or tune out all distractions as you drive. In this moment, just think. Ponder how you could be more. Achieve more. Leave a bigger mark on the world.

As Nocero asserts, "There is power in dreaming."

# -99-
# We Are One

Arguably the most intense and well-known college football rivalry is Army-Navy, as the interest in this game goes well beyond the students in those service academies.

What sets this game apart, however, is not the tradition of the game itself. Rather, as is tradition, following the game, despite the outcome, the two teams show their mutual respect by singing each other's fight song, signifying that together we are one – one military, standing as one nation.

Life is chock full of rivalries. Sports. Political. Corporate. Religious. Community. At some point, however, we cannot divvy up humanity into teams based on beliefs, race, or ethnicity. We are all human.

We need to stand together against hunger, disease, and natural disasters of every kind. We need to coordinate our knowledge to ensure the survival of this species. We need to do this so that one day, our children's', children's, children's can continue to proclaim, *We Are One*.

# -100-
# 1,000 Shots Made

On January 22, 2006, in what will always be known as one of the greatest single-game performances in NBA history, the late Kobe Bryant scored 81 points to help lead the Los Angeles Lakers to a 122-104 comeback victory at home over the Toronto Raptors.

Going 28-of-46 shooting, the media asked Bryant if he was surprised by his performance. He calmly responded:

"I wasn't surprised I scored 81 points to be honest with you. I trained eight hours a day - everyday. That's 1,000 made shots per day."

Bryant's point is that success doesn't materialize out of nowhere. Rather, it's preceded by hard work. For him it was working on his shot, day after day. For you, it's something else. Which begs the question: How are you honing your craft? What represents your metaphorical 1,000 shots a day?

## -101-
## Navigating a Maze From Within

Social architect Terry Bean remarked in his book *Be Connected* that often when he encounters others, they are not clear as to what sort of assistance they need. He goes on to share:

"These people are the ones who haven't done the work. They haven't taken the time to figure out what they seek. Not everyone knows what they want. And maybe they knew yesterday, but it changed. Life certainly has a way of getting in the way."

Bean elaborates that you can add great value to these people by helping them figure out what they should be looking for. It's as if they are navigating a maze from within. It's easy to be unclear as to whether one should go left or right.

But from your outside perspective you can help them become clear as to the direction they should go. This helps sets them up for future success. And they will remember you for that assistance.

**There you have it—101 essays. But we wanted to offer a bonus essay. Before we do, if you're interested in exploring other books, content, and programs by Frank Agin, visit frankagin.com or simply search "Frank Agin" on whatever platform you use to get great content.**

# -102-
# A Magnet of Positivity

In his book *The Power of Positivity: Controlling Where the Ball Bounces*, motivational speaker Cornell Thomas shares:

"I feel we are all magnets. You meet some people that always seem to have that rain cloud over their heads. They go through setback after setback until eventually they feel there' no hope for things to change. On the other hand, there are others who seem like the luckiest people in the world. Good fortune happens to them on daily basis, and it keeps happening. I started to realize that I could attract these great things just by staying positive."

Thomas is right. You can be a magnet of positivity. If you have positive thoughts, then positive things will come out of your mouth. And from that, you will carry yourself in a more positive manner. This leads to other positive people surrounding you, bringing their positive situations to you.

## About The Author

Frank Agin is president of AmSpirit Business Connections, which empowers entrepreneurs, sales representatives, and professionals to become successful and gain more referrals through networking.

He also shares information and insights on professional relationships, business networking and best practices for generating referrals on his Networking Rx podcast and through various professional programs.

Finally, Frank is the author of several books, including *Foundational Networking: Building Know, Like & Trust to Create a Life of Extraordinary Success*. See all his books and programs at frankagin.com. You can reach him at frankagin@amspirit.com.

www.ingramcontent.com/pod-product-compliance
Lightning Source LLC
Chambersburg PA
CBHW040757220326
41597CB00029BB/4964